For we are God's masterpiece.

He has created us anew in Christ Jesus,

so we can do the good things he

planned for us long ago.

—EPHESIANS 2:10 (NLT)

EACH DAY IS A GIFT FROM GOD, a blank canvas on which to begin anew. By greeting every morning with a palette filled with love, joy, kindness, patience, gentleness, and other fruits of the Spirit, we can make every day brighter.

When the Holy Spirit is at work within us, amazing things can happen, but as we toggle between our responsibilities, there is often little time to dedicate to ourselves and we can feel depleted. That's exactly when we need to take time to nourish ourselves—to lean on the Lord, to pray . . . and to play. With this book, you can do all of these things simultaneously.

Artist Lorrie Bennett designed the illustrations to glorify timeless scriptural lessons, providing a creative outlet for you to relax and reflect on God's Word. Each verse reminds us how acts of kindness and selflessness can make a difference, not only in our spiritual lives, but in the lives of others.

As you fill these pages with colors and patterns, it is our hope that you feel inspired and renewed, and that you reap the many blessings that come when you walk an inspired path.

But the fruit of the Spirit is love, joy, peace,

patience, kindness, goodness, faithfulness,

gentleness, self-control . . .

—GALATIANS 5:22–23 (NASB)

A Note from the Illustrator

A WARM HELLO FROM MY HEART TO YOURS. I am honored and humbled that I get to share my art with you. God is the ultimate Artist who designed our world and gave each of us unique gifts and talents. It is my hope that this book helps you reconnect with your artistic gifts or discover talents you didn't know you had.

My faith has been a touchstone in my life and I feel blessed to use my gifts to glorify God and inspire others. When I engage in any type of art, I feel more alive and yet relaxed at the same time. As you spend time with these pages, I hope that you feel recharged and renewed.

Each person will color each page differently. Allow yourself to try out new color palettes, techniques, or materials. Most of all, have fun, create, and celebrate your faith.

—Wishing You Colorful Blessings,
Lorrie Bennett

LORRIE BENNETT *is blessed to live her life as an artist, crafter, teacher, graphic designer, and best of all, a mother. She is passionate about the divine inspiration that is the source of her creativity, and the happiness that it can bring to others. Visit www.dzineafterhours.blogspot.com*

Try These Techniques

COLORING IS SUPPOSED TO BE A STRESS-FREE, no-worries kind of activity. There really is no right or wrong way to do it. But for anyone who wants to make each page come alive, here are some tips.

BLENDING COLORS—By blending several colors together, you can create a three-dimensional shading effect. For example, if you want to color a leaf green, use the color wheel on the next page to choose several shades of green as well as some colors next to the green (yellows and blues). Try to envision where the light would be falling on your image. Wherever the light would fall on the leaf is where you will place your lightest colors (the lighter greens and yellow). Wherever the shadow would fall is where you would place your darker colors (the darker green and a bit of blue). By overlapping the colors and blending them, you will create a realistic effect. It helps to practice on a piece of scrap paper first, and to work slowly to see if you are creating the effect you wish before you complete a large area.

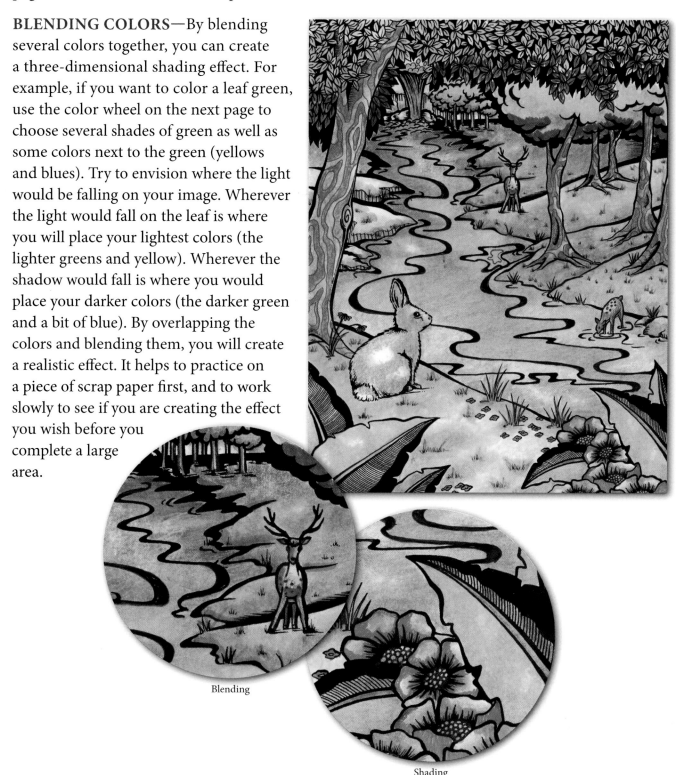

Blending

Shading

Coloring Tips & Tools

COLORED PENCILS: great for shading or blending colors together, both of which add interest and depth to any design.

GEL PENS AND MARKERS: good for adding bold, defined bursts of color.

CRAYONS: surprisingly versatile when filling in large spaces.

TIP: Add a piece of scrap paper under each page you're working on to make sure that the ink doesn't bleed through the page.

Choose Your Colors

PRIMARY COLORS
The primary colors—red, yellow, and blue—are denoted by a "P" on the outside of the color wheel. Primary colors cannot be created by mixing any other colors.

SECONDARY COLORS
The secondary colors— green, orange, and purple—are shown by an "S" on the color wheel. These are formed by mixing the primary colors.

TERTIARY COLORS
Yellow-orange, red-orange, red-purple, blue-purple, blue-green, and yellow-green make up the tertiary colors, which are noted with a "T" on the outside of the wheel. These colors are formed by mixing a primary color with a secondary color.

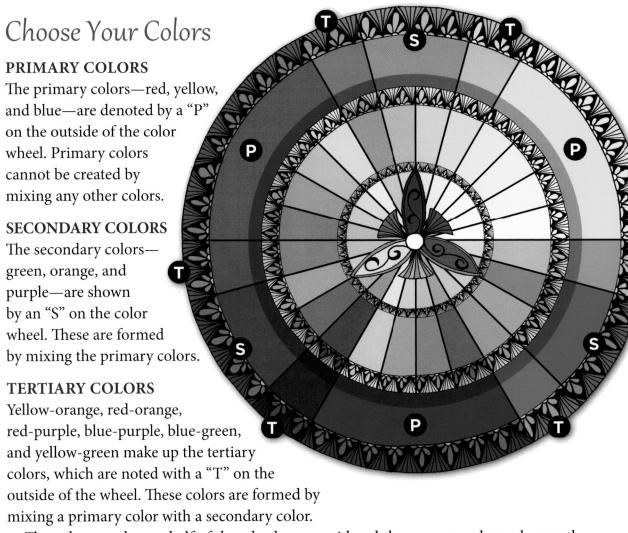

The colors on the top half of the wheel are considered the warmer colors whereas the bottom hues are the cooler ones. Colors that fall opposite of one another on the wheel are complementary, and the ones that fall next to each other are analogous. You can use both complementary and analogous colors to make a gorgeous piece of art—the possibilities are as endless as your imagination.

I have set my rainbow in the clouds, and it will be the

sign of the covenant between me and the earth.

—GENESIS 9:13 (NIV)

Harmony How-Tos

NOT SURE OF WHAT COLORS TO USE? You can find a rainbow of inspiration around you in the patterns of plants, animals, flowers, sunsets, or the morning sky.

A nature-inspired color scheme with analogous colors

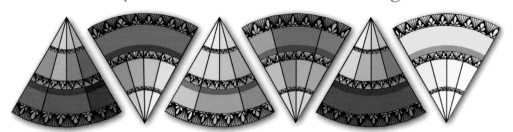

ANALOGOUS COLORS are any three colors which are side by side on a 12-part color wheel, such as yellow-green, yellow, and yellow-orange or teal blue, blue, and indigo.

A nature-inspired color scheme with complementary colors

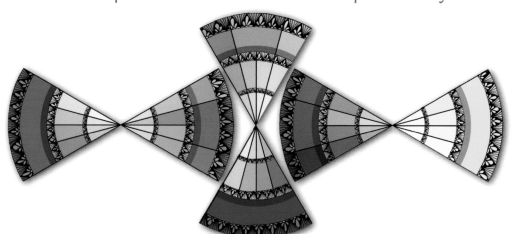

COMPLEMENTARY COLORS are any two colors which are directly opposite each other, such as yellow and purple or orange and blue.

Warm colors   Cool colors   Analogous colors   Complementary colors

Pick Your Palette

Having a hard time picking your palette? Try some of these color combinations. You can also find many resources online or by looking at the color palettes in nature.

COTTON CANDY APPLE

MONOCHROME MOCHAS

MELLOW YELLOW

JEWEL TONES

SUNRISE

PEACOCK

Use the following colored pages as your inspiration. Happy coloring!

Colored pencil art by Amanda Collins.

Digital art by Lawna Patterson Oldfield.

Marker art by Robyn Henoch.

Crayon art by Tyler Blonshine.

Marker art by Robyn Henoch.

Marker and colored pencil art by Lawna Patterson Oldfield.

Marker art by Marina Koustas.

Marker art by Robyn Henoch.

Love is patient, love is kind.

It does not envy, it does not boast,

it is not proud. It does not dishonor

others, it is not self-seeking,

it is not easily angered,

it keeps no record of wrongs.

—1 CORINTHIANS 13:4–5 (NIV)

Let the peace of Christ rule in your hearts,

since as members of one body

you were called to peace.

And be thankful.

—COLOSSIANS 3:15 (NIV)

I can do all things through Him

who strengthens me.

—PHILIPPIANS 4:13 (NASB)

Therefore, as God's chosen people,

holy and dearly loved, clothe yourselves with compassion,

kindness, humility, gentleness and patience.

Bear with each other and forgive one another if any

of you has a grievance against someone.

Forgive as the Lord forgave you.

And over all these virtues put on love, which

binds them all together in perfect unity.

—COLOSSIANS 3:12–13 (NIV)

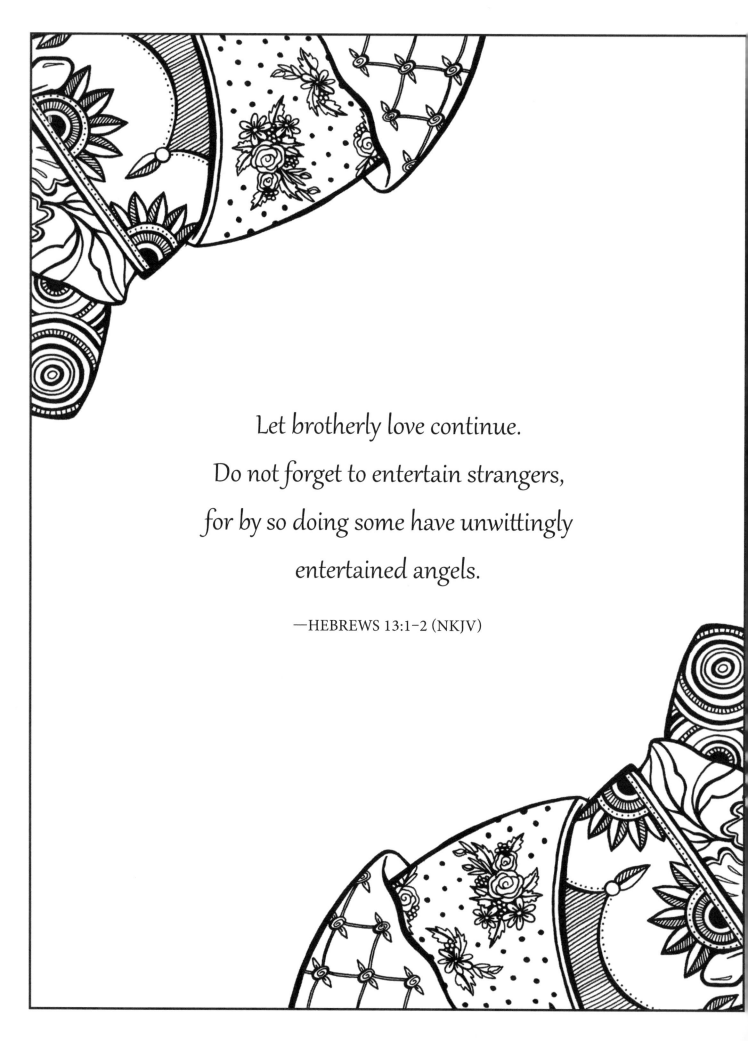

Let brotherly love continue.
Do not forget to entertain strangers,
for by so doing some have unwittingly
entertained angels.

—HEBREWS 13:1–2 (NKJV)

Do not FORGET to Entertain STRANGERS ...... for by so doing SOME have unwittingly entertained Angels

— Hebrews 13:2

If I take part in the meal with thankfulness,

why am I denounced because of

something I thank God for?

So whether you eat or drink or whatever you do,

do it all for the glory of God.

—1 CORINTHIANS 10:30–31 (NIV)

Make a joyful noise to the LORD, all the earth;

break forth into joyous song and sing praises!

Sing praises to the LORD with the lyre,

with the lyre and the sound of melody!

With trumpets and the sound of the horn

make a joyful noise before the King, the LORD!

—PSALM 98:4–6 (ESV)

I am the vine; you are the branches.

If you remain in me and I in you, you will bear much fruit;

apart from me you can do nothing. If you do not remain in me,

you are like a branch that is thrown away and withers;

such branches are picked up, thrown into the fire and burned.

If you remain in me and my words remain in you,

ask whatever you wish, and it will be done for you.

—JOHN 15:5–6 (NIV)

I am
the vine;
you are the
branches

John 15:5

For this reason I remind you to fan into flame
the gift of God, which is in you through the laying on
of my hands, for God gave us a spirit not of fear
but of power and love and self-control.

—2 TIMOTHY 1:6–7 (ESV)

For God gave us a SPIRIT not of fear

but of POWER and LOVE and SELF-CONTROL

2 Timothy 1:7

I lift up my eyes to the mountains—

where does my help come from?

My help comes from the LORD,

the Maker of heaven and earth.

—PSALM 121: 1–2 (NIV)

I LIFT MY EYES
UP TO THE
MOUNTAINS ~
WHERE DOES
MY HELP
COME FROM?

PSALM 121:1-2

Let your gentleness be evident to all.

The Lord is near.

—PHILIPPIANS 4:5 (NIV)

But the fruit of the Spirit is love, joy,

peace, patience, kindness, goodness, faithfulness,

gentleness, and self-control.

Against such things there is no law.

—GALATIANS 5:22–23 (NASB)

but THE FRUIT OF THE SPIRIT is

LOVE
Galatians 5:22
joy
PEACE
PATIENCE
goodness
joy
kind ness
faithfulness
gentleness AND
SELF CONTROL

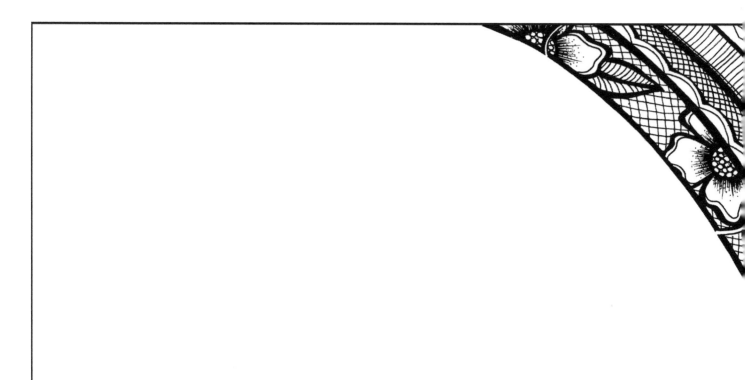

Your word is a lamp to my feet

and a light to my path.

—PSALM 119:105 (NKJV)

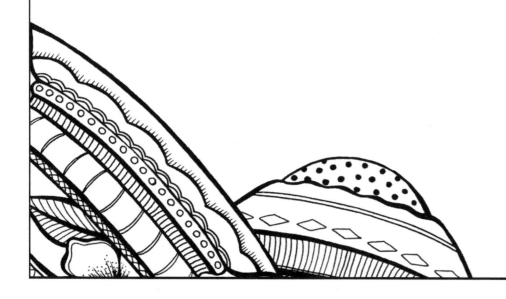

Be watchful, stand firm in the faith,

act like men, be strong.

Let all that you do be done in love.

—1 CORINTHIANS 16:13–14 (ESV)

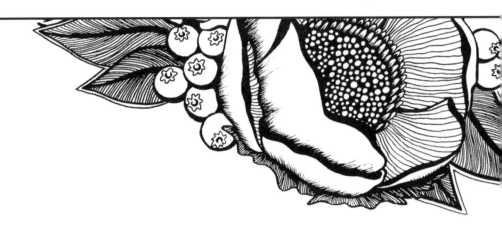

Sing praise to the LORD, you His godly ones,

And give thanks to His holy name.

For His anger is but for a moment,

His favor is for a lifetime;

Weeping may last for the night,

But a shout of joy comes in the morning.

—PSALM 30:4–5 (NASB)

For I am confident of this very thing,

that He who began a good work in you will

perfect it until the day of Christ Jesus.

—PHILIPPIANS 1:6 (NASB)

Be Patient

God is not finished with me yet.

For who is God except the LORD?

Who but our God is a solid rock?

God arms me with strength,

and he makes my way perfect.

He makes me as surefooted as a deer,

enabling me to stand on mountain heights.

—PSALM 18:31–33 (NLT)

He makes me as surefooted as a deer, enabling me to stand on mountain heights.

Psalm 18:33

And now, just as you accepted Christ Jesus
as your Lord, you must continue to follow him.
Let your roots grow down into him,
and let your lives be built on him.
Then your faith will grow strong in the truth
you were taught, and you will
overflow with thankfulness.

—COLOSSIANS 2:6–7 (NLT)

There is no fear in love,

but perfect love casts out fear.

For fear has to do with punishment, and

whoever fears has not been perfected in love.

We love because he first loved us.

—1 JOHN 4:18–19 (ESV)

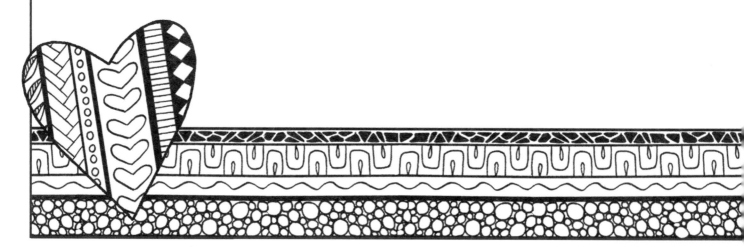

WE love because He FIRST loved US

1 John 4:19

My dear brothers and sisters, take note of this:

Everyone should be quick to listen,

slow to speak and slow to become angry.

—JAMES 1:19 (NIV)

Trust in the LORD with all your heart

And do not lean on your own understanding.

In all your ways acknowledge Him,

And He will make your paths straight.

—PROVERBS 3:5–6 (NASB)

PROVERBS 3:5-6

The generous man will be prosperous,

And he who waters will himself be watered.

—PROVERBS 11:25 (NASB)

Blessed
ARE THE MEEK FOR THEY SHALL
inherit the earth
MATTHEW 5:5

Rejoice in the Lord always. I will say it again: Rejoice!

Let your gentleness be evident to all.

The Lord is near. Do not be anxious about anything,

but in every situation, by prayer and petition,

with thanksgiving,

present your requests to God.

—PHILIPPIANS 4:4–6 (NIV)

REJOICE

IN THE

Lord

ALWAYS

Philippians 4:4

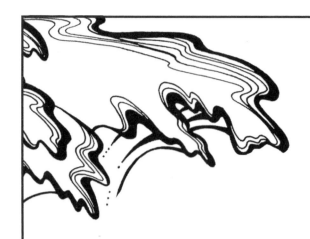

Mightier than the thunder of the great waters,

mightier than the breakers of the sea—

the LORD on high is mighty.

—PSALM 93:4 (NIV)

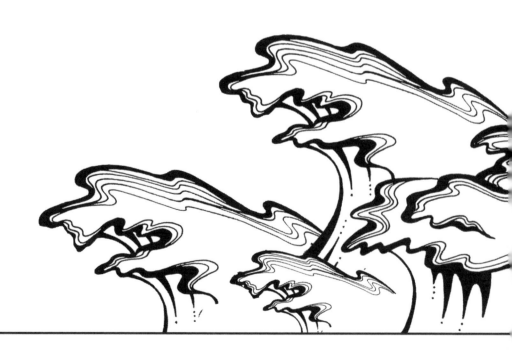

Whatever house you enter, first say,

"Peace be to this house!"

And if a son of peace is there, your peace

will rest upon him.

But if not, it will return to you.

—LUKE 10:5–6 (ESV)

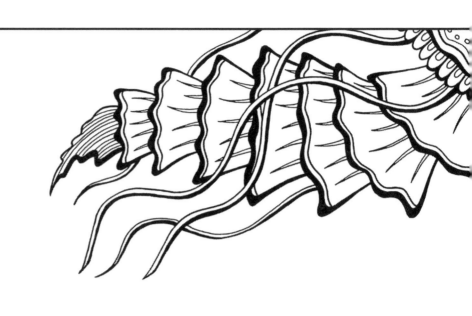

When you go through deep waters,

I will be with you.

When you go through rivers of difficulty,

you will not drown.

—ISAIAH 43:2 (NLT)

when you go
through
deep waters
I will be
with you
Isaiah 43:2

How precious is your unfailing love, O God!

All humanity finds shelter in the shadow of your wings.

You feed them from the abundance of your own house,

letting them drink from your river of delights.

For you are the fountain of life,

the light by which we see.

—PSALM 36:7–9 (NLT)

How precious is your UNFAILING *Love*, O God!

Psalm 36:7

ALL HUMANITY FINDS SHELTER IN THE SHADOW OF YOUR WINGS.

The grass withers and the flowers fade,

but the word of our God will stand forever.

—ISAIAH 40:8 (NLT)

For the LORD God is a sun and shield;

The LORD will give grace and glory;

No good thing will He withhold

From those who walk uprightly.

—PSALM 84:11 (NKJV)